UEA MA Creati
Anthologies 20
Scriptwriting

UEA SCRIPTWRITING 2015

First published by Egg Box Publishing 2015

International © 2015 retained by individual authors.

This book is sold subject to the condition that it shall not, by way of trade or otherwise, be lent, resold, hired out, stored in a retrieval system, or otherwise circulated without the publisher's prior consent in any form of binding or cover other than that in which it is published and without a similar condition including this condition being imposed on the subsequent purchaser.

A CIP record for this book is available from the British Library.

UEA SCRIPTWRITING 2015 is typeset in Adobe Garamond. Titles are set in Mercury.

Cover photography from the photographic unit, UEA.

Printed and bound in the UK by Imprint Digital.

Designed and typeset by Sean Purdy.

Proofread by Sarah Gooderson.

Distributed by Central Books.

ISBN: 978-0-9932962-4-6

Acknowledgements

Thanks are due to the School of Literature, Drama and Creative Writing at UEA in partnership with Egg Box Publishing for making the UEA MA Creative Writing anthologies possible.

We'd also like to thank the following people:

Tiffany Atkinson, John Boyne, Andrew Cowan,
Helen Cross, Giles Foden, Sarah Gooderson,
Rachel Hore, Kathryn Hughes, Catrina Laskey,
Bill Manhire, Jean McNeil, Natalie Mitchell,
Jeremy Noel-Tod, Beatrice Poubeau, Rob Ritchie,
Sophie Robinson, Helen Smith, Henry Sutton,
Val Taylor, Ian Thomson, Steve Waters,
Frances Wilson and Peter Womack.

Nathan Hamilton at Egg Box Publishing, and Sean Purdy.

Editorial team:

Rob Atkinson
Sohini Basak
Gill Blanchard
Jemma Carter
Joanna Graham
Alexis Kuzma
Elizabeth Lewis-Williams
Emma Victoria Miller
Molly Morris
Kayla Schmidt
Jade Tremblay
Chloe L Yeoh

CONTENTS

Introduction —————————————— 07
Steve Waters

Contributors:

Dominic Croucher ————————————— 13
Uno

Edward Dyer ——————————————— 31
Racing Hearts

Mariama Ives-Moiba ————————————— 39
Three Bridesmaids,
a Snickers and a Bathtub

Tom Lashley ——————————————— 49
Time's Up

Mark Probert ——————————————— 57
Bairstow-Minghella

Michelle Sewell ——————————————— 69
The Tinder Game

Jade Tremblay ——————————————— 87
Too Old For This

Amy Whitington ——————————————— 97
The Clockmaker's Wife

STEVE WATERS

Introduction

WELCOME TO THE 2015 ANTHOLOGY OF MA CREATIVE WRITING: Scriptwriting. Its contents reveal where we are coming from: no rules but good writing obtain; detail is king. These pages contain a tour of the horizon of what dramatic writing might be right now. Interested in a verbatim look at digital love? Michelle Sewell's trawl through Tinder might be for you. Fancy a glance at tragedy through the prism of point of view? Edward Dyer's and Tom Lashley's short films deliver that in telling detail. Or maybe you favour farce reinvented or satire rebooted? Well, Mariama Ives-Moiba's hilarious tale of bridesmaids stuck in a Hummer or Mark Probert's dead-eyed dissection of corporate blah might do the trick. OK, how about close-up human drama, tales of the woe that is marriage or of hurts hidden by blokeish banter: check out Jade Tremblay for the former or Dominic Croucher for the latter. Or if you're more in the mood for a little steampunk magic realism, I refer you to Amy Whitington's gorgeous tale of clockmakers.

Eight writers, eight distinct worlds, genres and eight ideas of what writing now might be; eight voices from as far afield as Australia and Canada, from different generations and in different media. Diversity for us is always the key; but not out of an attitude of 'anything goes', more from a sense that each writer finds their own landscape and locates the right form with which to map it. But equally, these works all speak to the power of the short form: punchy acts of story-telling, shapely slices of life. What a writer can do in ten minutes tells us as much as what they can pull off in ninety. If, as Jonathan Franzen once said, 'there is no hiding place in the short story,' then there's even less in the short play or film where every line and gesture must earn its keep. Goethe suggested that the devil is in the detail, but I suspect God might be lurking in there too.

And when I think of detail, I think of the vigilant, insightful dramaturgical gaze of my colleague Val Taylor for whom this is her final year as MA convenor. For two decades Val has been the face of Scriptwriting, forging a community of talent within and beyond the campus, nurturing writers of afternoon plays for radio, returning TV series, sci-fi blockbusters, searing in-yer-face plays, sit-coms, rom-coms and more. In my three years alongside her, I have learned so much from witnessing her unrelenting attention and commitment to detail. Both Brecht and Hardy sought to be remembered as writers who 'noticed things'; Val's teaching and this compendium of fleeting dramas share that crucial aspiration.

Steve Waters, May 2015

UEA MA Creative Writing Anthologies 2015: Scriptwriting

DOMINIC CROUCHER

Uno

INT. HOSPITAL – NIGHT

The paediatric ward is empty except for two teenagers. Ewan (14, gaunt and skinny) lies in bed, playing cards with Jimmy (15, clearly healthier) who sits in a chair by Ewan's bed.

Jimmy takes a sip from a cup of water, pausing for effect.

Ewan hangs on his every word.

                  JIMMY
    Spank it everywhere, mate. It'll hit a ton in third.
    Every lunch we used to go round and get orders
    from all the year elevens, then me and Angela – you
    know Angela…

Jimmy indicates large breasts. Ewan grins.

                JIMMY (CONT'D)
    We'd spank it up to McDonald's in ten minutes flat.
    Pick everything up, spank it back. Made stacks, bro.
    But this one time I was coming down the A28, right,
    and the LAPD started flashing the blues and twos
    behind me.

                EWAN
    Did you spank it?

                    JIMMY
    Not a fuckin' amateur, mate. I pull over, right, and
    just as he comes to my door I get all panicked, like
    'Ahh, you gotta help me, my girlfriend's havin' a
    baby! I gotta get to the hospital!'

Ewan looks awestruck.

Another sip. Another pause.

                    EWAN
    And?!

                    JIMMY
    He shits himself. Gave me a personal escort right up
    to the door. Just sat in the hospital and waited for
    him to do one.

                    EWAN
    They never found out?

                    JIMMY
    Nah! Police ain't too smart, Ewan.

Jimmy places his cards down on top of Ewan's and knocks over his cup of water as Steve (16) enters.

Steve carries a backpack and looks sullen.

                    JIMMY (CONT'D)
    Oi oi! What you doin' here?

Steve ignores him.

He crosses the room and dumps his bag on an empty bed. He starts unpacking.

EWAN

Hi, Steve.

STEVE

All right?

EWAN

Yeah.

JIMMY

They kick you out when they found out your balls haven't dropped yet? Or did you start pissing the bed again?

STEVE

Fuck off.

JIMMY

Only bants. Only Banter Clause. Only the Archbishop of Banterbury—

STEVE

Fuck off!

JIMMY

Here, Steve, sort this out. You know, like, when you die, your face freezes?

STEVE

What?

JIMMY

Like, when you die the face you pull is frozen on and that's your face forever.

STEVE

No.

                    JIMMY
          We've been practising. Tell us whose is better.

Jimmy motions at Ewan.

Ewan folds his arms across his chest and smiles, peacefully.

                    JIMMY (CONT'D)
          Nah, you want more like…

Jimmy clamps his arms to his side and gurns like a moron.

                    STEVE
          Such a pleb.

                    JIMMY
          How very dare you?

                    STEVE
          Sorry. You're a Plebasaurus rex. Bants.

                    JIMMY
          Fine. If that's the way you wanna play it, you won't
          be getting your present.

                    EWAN
          Aww, come on, Jim!

                    STEVE
          What present?

                    EWAN
          Let him see, go on!

Jimmy pretends to consider the request.
He moves to his bedside drawer, rummages around in the bottom and pulls out a soggy, flaccid cannabis joint. It's a pretty sorry sight.

STEVE

What the fuck is that?

EWAN

He nicked it!

STEVE

From who?

JIMMY

Can't tell you, mate. A dealer never reveals his secrets.

EWAN

No, you never reveal your secrets.

JIMMY

Good lad.

STEVE

This is a joke, right? You're not putting that inside you?

JIMMY

I never joke. Even about what's been inside you. And calm down, it's just gear.

EWAN

Just gear, man.

STEVE

It's illegal.

JIMMY

What's the worst that could happen?

STEVE

You could die.

Beat.

> JIMMY
> Good thing I'm in a hospital then.

> STEVE
> Fuck this, do what you want.

Steve gets into bed, connects his IV drip and turns away from them.

Jimmy lights the joint and takes an elaborate drag. He tries and fails to blow smoke rings, then hands the joint to Ewan.

Ewan takes a drag and coughs. Jimmy smiles knowingly and takes the joint back.

A few tokes later...

> JIMMY
> Would you rather have, like, an arm coming out of your forehead, or a leg for a tail?

> EWAN
> How big is my tail leg? Can I call it my teg?

> JIMMY
> Call it what you want, mate, but it's fucking massive. You have to get special trousers made, but on the plus side, you can sleep standing up. I suppose the arm would be good for if you got in a fight. Ahhh, this one time, right, me and Mars Bar – you know Mars Bar, the guy who ate three hundred Mars Bars in an hour and then had to have his stomach pumped and now he can only eat lettuce – we were down the White Lion and this big bloke come up to us and—

> EWAN
> How big?

JIMMY

What?

EWAN

How big was he?

JIMMY

You know André the Giant?

EWAN

Mmm.

JIMMY

Bigger.

EWAN

Woah.

JIMMY

Yep. Anyway, so I was… wait, what was I…

EWAN

D'you think there's a Ewan the Giant?

JIMMY

Nah, before that, what was it?

EWAN

Something about lemons?

JIMMY

Oh yeah. So me and my mate Stig – you know Stig, the one who used to race Formula 1 cars but gave it up to go into his dad's used lighter sales business – me and Stig ate fifty lemons and then the next day all of our hair went yellow.

EWAN

Serious?

JIMMY

No lie.

Steve turns to face them.

Enough is enough.

STEVE

Bull shit.

JIMMY

I'm tellin' ya.

STEVE

So you ate fifty lemons and your hair instantly went yellow.

JIMMY

Nah, it took a few hours.

STEVE

Course.

EWAN

Does anyone wanna play cards?

STEVE

You're so full of shit!

JIMMY

Don't hate, man.

STEVE

And stop fucking talking like that! You're not some LA gangster.

                    JIMMY
    Word.

                    EWAN
    Or we could play Uno?

                    STEVE
    I'm trying to fucking sleep!

Steve turns away from them and pulls his blanket over his head.

Jimmy catches Ewan's eye and sneaks over to Steve's bed. He tips some of the weed from the joint into Steve's IV bag.

Ewan giggles.

Jimmy throws him a warning look, but it's too late – Steve has noticed.

Jimmy throws himself against the wall.

                    STEVE (CONT'D)
    What you doing?

                    JIMMY
    Stretching.

Jimmy raises a solitary arm into the air.

                    STEVE
    D'you know how much shit you'll get in when they
    find out about this?

                    JIMMY
    They won't find out.
                    EWAN
    Yeah, they won't find out.

                    STEVE
        It's bad enough you doing it, but forcing him...

Steve's speech starts to slur.

                    STEVE (CONT'D)
        I thought you had some fucking sense.

A grin creeps over Steve's face before he catches himself.

                    STEVE (CONT'D)
        What the fuck have you done?

                    JIMMY
        Nothing.

                    EWAN
        Ain't done nothing!

Steve rips his IV from his arm and walks towards Ewan's bed. He notices the crumbled cannabis in his IV.

                    STEVE
        This is bullshit! Why'd you do that? You fucking
        arsehole, you fucking twat!

                    JIMMY
        Why are you speaking in rhymes? You're not an LA
        rapper, bro.

                    EWAN
        Not a rapper, bro.

                    STEVE
        I'm not rhyming, I don't know how. I'll stop
        rhyming, I'll stop it now.

Steve looks horrified. He has no control over this. It's Christmas come early for Ewan and Jimmy.

                      JIMMY
Steve, what's the food like in the adult ward?

                      STEVE
                      (Raps)
It's amazing, tantalising, ridiculous, incredible. Everything you see and hear and smell is surely edible. The shit they throw together here is so bland, but upstairs every single meal is pre-planned. You eat five times a day to keep up your weight. And they serve it to you on a proper china plate. None of those stupid paper cups, they're a calamity. I think they use them here to preserve familiarity. They treat the kids like dogs, it's a travesty, when we're all just the same in this vicinity—

                      EWAN
That doesn't rhyme.

Steve breaks out of the trance.

                      STEVE
Oh yeah. What is that stuff?

                      JIMMY
Never reveal your sources.

                      EWAN
Never reveal your sources.

                      JIMMY
Good lad. Right, would you rather talk like Terminator or Barry Scott for the rest of your life?

                      STEVE
Who?

JIMMY

What is actually wrong with you? Are you mental? He's the Cillit Bang guy. Always talks like he's being probed, like –

(Impersonates Barry Scott)
'Hi, I'm Barry Scott, buy this cleaning shit 'cause if you don't a big man follows me round with a glove on one hand and a weird look in his eye.'

STEVE

(Sarcastically)
Tough choice.

EWAN

Mmm. You met him, Jim?

JIMMY

Yeah, I was giving some business classes up London with Dingo – you know Dingo, he's the one who lived with wolves until he was fourteen and then got recruited by the army to teach the SAS combat skills – and he come up to us and started begging me to flog his shit. I said, 'Baz, you wanna know the secret to success?' He says, 'Yeah', I says, 'Don't sell the shit. Let the shit sell you.' Boom.

EWAN

Woah.

STEVE

You don't actually believe any of this do you?

EWAN

Jim's well good with stuff like this.

JIMMY

True dat.

STEVE
Stop fucking doing that! Dat is a bunch of bollocks.

JIMMY
No it ain't!

EWAN
It ain't!

STEVE
I don't know how you do it, you don't even have your MA in Bullshit Studies.

JIMMY
Is that like General Studies?

EWAN
I'm sure Jim could go to uni if he wanted to.

STEVE
Oh my God, you've got to stop listening to him!

JIMMY
As if!

STEVE
He's turning into a mini version of you, he can't even think for himself any more!

JIMMY
Bollocks.

EWAN
Yeah, bollocks.

Beat.

JIMMY
All right, Ewan, what do you wanna do?

EWAN
We could have a sword fight?

STEVE
What are we, six?

EWAN
I never had one.

STEVE
Sure you had much better things to do when you were six.

EWAN
I was here.

JIMMY
OK, here we go…

Jimmy picks up two used rolls of wrapping paper. He tosses one to Ewan who prepares to attack him from his bed.

JIMMY (CONT'D)
Wait, what you doing? You can't kill me if your sword doesn't have a name. I'm pretty sure that's illegal, actually.

STEVE
Erm…

JIMMY
Mine's Excalibur. What's yours called?

EWAN
Um, Mildred.

Jimmy shrugs and begins to play-fight with Ewan.

Steve watches as Jimmy dances around Ewan's bed, Ewan's face alive with childlike glee.

Steve's expression softens.

Jimmy lets Ewan stab him and makes a meal of dying on the floor.

Steve takes a pack of Uno cards from his backpack and deals them into three piles on Ewan's bedside table.

Jimmy gets up, turns on the TV (Disney's *Frozen* is playing) and sits on Ewan's bed to play Uno.

Steve and Jimmy seem to be letting Ewan win.

                    EWAN (CONT'D)
Uno!

                    JIMMY
In France, it's actually pronounced you-know.

                    EWAN
          (To Steve)
Really?

                    STEVE
Er, sometimes, yeah.

                    EWAN
You-know!

                    JIMMY
He knows.

Steve gestures to the TV.

                    STEVE
I can't stand this shite.

                        JIMMY
            Ah, thank you!

                        EWAN
            It's not that bad.

Steve hears the song *Do You Wanna Build a Snowman* on the TV.

                        STEVE
            Do I wanna build a snowman? No I fucking don't,
            leave me alone.

Ewan's eyelids start to droop.

                        JIMMY
            This bloke come up to me once and tried to sell me a
            snowman.

                        STEVE
            Did you batter him?

                        JIMMY
            Yeah, I battered him.

Ewan is all but asleep now.

                        JIMMY (CONT'D)
            Good shit, right?

Steve offers half a smile.

                        EWAN
            I like music.

                        JIMMY
            Thanks for contributing, big man.

EWAN
But I don't get it. How can you be not not knocking on heaven's door?

STEVE
You'll have to ask the other big man.

EWAN
Won't be long.

JIMMY
What?

EWAN
Six...

STEVE
Years?

Ewan shakes his head, no.

JIMMY
Six months?

Ewan shakes his head again.

JIMMY (CONT'D)
It's not my brain. It's my balls.

STEVE
Must be all the shagging.

Beat.

STEVE (CONT'D)
You know...

                    JIMMY
You know…

                    EWAN
Yeah, I know.

Dominic Croucher chose to pursue Scriptwriting after completing a degree in marketing. So far, he is enjoying unemployment. He writes primarily for film and has recently become involved in a charity which raises awareness for those who suffer (like him) from having taken General Studies at 'A' Level.

EDWARD DYER

Racing Hearts

FADE IN:

INT. JACK'S BEDROOM – AUTUMN, PRESENT DAY, EARLY MORNING

Light shines through the window. The bedroom is messy and filled with all manner of racing posters, toys and duvet covers. There is a large poster of Ayrton Senna above the bed. JACK (10) is standing in front of a full-length mirror. His mother, CAROL (34), is brushing down the white shirt he's wearing. They both look in the mirror. Jack smiles; Carol is close to tears.

FLASHBACK

INT. HALLWAY – NIGHT

Carol is sitting on the stairs, caught in the faint light of the TV, casting shadows of the banisters over her face. She's been crying for an hour and can't shed any more tears.

The kitchen light along the corridor is bright. There's a man's coat hanging off the back of one of the chairs, and a baby's bottle of milk on the counter.

FLASHBACK

INT. HALLWAY – EARLIER, EVENING

Jack is standing in his race car pyjamas at the top of the stairs. Somewhere in the kitchen below, a glass smashes. Jack doesn't react. He can see long shadows along the hallway. Carol and JONATHAN (38), his father, are arguing.

> JONATHAN
> You think my job is easy?

> CAROL
> I never said that.

> JONATHAN
> Nine 'til five. Every day for the last seven years. I've sacrificed everything.

> CAROL
> So have I.

> JONATHAN
> Like what? You'd never blame yourself for any of this, would you? Of course, this is all my fault!

Jack puts his hands over his ears.

> CAROL
> (inaudible)
> You're not even listening to me.

> JONATHAN
> (inaudible)
> I'm going out. I need a drink.

> CAROL
> (inaudible)
> No you don't. You don't…

                          JONATHAN
                          (inaudible)
                    I'm taking the car. Don't wait up.

Jonathan pulls on his coat, leaves the kitchen and exits the house through the front door. Upstairs, Jack's sister ELLA (18 months) begins to cry. Carol stirs in the kitchen. It's only then that Jack runs back to his room.

EXT. DRIVEWAY – PRESENT DAY, EARLY MORNING

Jack, wearing a dark suit jacket over his shirt and a badly fastened black tie, is ushered out of the front door. He is holding Ella's hand, who toddles beside him. Carol, wearing a black veil, turns to shut the front door to their semi-detached house, but drops the keys in her struggle to find the right one.

Jack and Ella walk down the tarmacked driveway towards a black limousine. JEAN (70) and BILLY (68), Carol's parents, help the children and their mother into the car. They too are wearing dark clothes.

INT. LIMOUSINE – CONTINUOUS

Jack looks out of the window, as the door shuts, to watch the wind blow several leaves off an oak tree in their front garden.

                                              FLASHBACK

Jonathan, Carol, Jack and Ella (8 months) are having a picnic beneath some trees in a large park. Jonathan is drinking a bottle of Stella from a four-pack. The day is bright, but the air seems a little cold. There is a fenced playground behind them and a small stream in front where a few children are splashing in the water.

Jack plays with a blue, remote-controlled car. It moves quickly over the short grass on the field by the playground. Jonathan is helping him steer. Ella is in a basket, sucking her dummy, on the picnic blanket with Carol who is eating a cucumber sandwich. Ella drops the dummy and Jonathan turns back when she starts crying. Jack loses control of the car and it veers into a bush.

He looks over to the picnic and watches Jonathan try to soothe Ella. He can't and he passes her to Carol. He walks away. Jack shields his eyes from the sun, watching Jonathan go.

INT. FUNCTION ROOMS, 3-STAR HOTEL – PRESENT DAY, LATE MORNING

Jack looks up to lots of MOURNERS standing around the room, dressed all in black. They're standing in small groups around small card tables, against the bar and around the buffet table on the other side of the room. He glances over at Carol; she is holding Jean's hand and crying.

FLASHBACK

INT. SCHOOL CLASSROOM – AFTERNOON

During an art lesson, Jack is drawing a picture of a race car. It is surprisingly good for a 10-year-old. Two BOYS (10-11) are fighting next to him, and accidently knock Jack. A tin of red paint spills over his drawing and drips onto his uniform. The boys laugh. Jack stands up, furious, and pushes one of them back. He falls backwards onto the floor. MS ATHERTON (36), the art teacher, notices and strides over.

EXT. CHURCH YARD – PRESENT DAY, EARLY MORNING

The limousine pulls up outside a church. More autumn leaves fall and swirl in the courtyard.

FLASHBACK

INT. JACK'S BEDROOM – LATE EVENING

Jack is sitting on the edge of his bed, playing with his fingers. There is still red paint over his uniform. There is a half-eaten sandwich on a plate on the bed and a packet of unopened crisps.

Jonathan enters and tries to make Jack laugh by pulling a funny face. He walks, unsteadily, a little drunk, and sits down next to his son. They sit in silence.

Jonathan looks up at the poster of Ayrton Senna and then down to the plate of food on the bed. He opens the crisps and eats one. He offers one to Jack, who doesn't look up. Jonathan wipes his fingers on his trousers and gets up. He finds the remote control for the blue toy car. He drives it along the floor and steers into Jack's foot. He makes the car butt Jack's foot again and again. Jack smiles.

INT. CHURCH – PRESENT DAY, EARLY MORNING

Jack is staring at a RELATIVE at the lectern beside the coffin. She sobs at the end of her speech and then steps down. Billy gets up to comfort her. All that Jack can hear is the sniffling and suppressed sobbing of the other mourners.

FLASHBACK

INT. KITCHEN – EARLY AFTERNOON

Even though it is early, all of the lights are on in the house. Jonathan is sitting at the kitchen table, surrounded by scraps of paper, receipts and a calculator. He adds a few numbers together, but his attention is caught between the receipts and the tempting bottle of whisky. He squeezes his eyes to try and wake himself up.

He looks down at Jack's blue race car that has butted into his foot. Jonathan smiles at his son, standing in the doorway. He puts down his pen, grabs the bottle of whisky and heads out of the back door into the garden with Jack.

INT. JACK'S BEDROOM – LATER

Jack is sitting on the floor, hugging his duvet around him. There is a sliver of light coming in through his door from the hallway.

CAROL
Why can't you take this seriously?

                    JONATHAN
It sounds like you're blaming me for this. I work
hard all day, and you...

                    CAROL
I'm not blaming anyone.

                    JONATHAN
You sit at home all day. What have you got to show
for it?

                    CAROL
That's what we agreed. I'd stay home to look after
the kids.

                    JONATHAN
You've never thought I was a good father. I've never
been able to shut her up when she's crying.

                    CAROL
I don't want to lose my home.

Pans clatter. Ella starts crying in a room nearby; it goes unnoticed. Jack looks over to his race car.

INT. CHURCH – PRESENT DAY, EARLY MORNING

Jack looks either side of where he is sitting on the church pew. Some of his relatives are crying, holding hands. Others are smiling with fond memories, or looking away. He stares at the coffin.

INT. FUNCTION ROOM – PRESENT DAY, LATER

Jack is sitting alone. The mourners tuck into the buffet. Various relatives attempt to talk to him, but he doesn't hear them speak. Carol offers him some food: a sandwich and a packet of crisps. She leaves them on the table nearby, but they go untouched.

FLASHBACK

INT. KITCHEN – LATE EVENING

Jack is racing his blue car around the floor. Ella is sitting on a mat, playing with building blocks. The radio plays *Love Me Tender* by Elvis Presley, which is louder than the rain outside. Carol is washing up after dinner, ignoring the untouched plate of food still left on the table.

The front door swings open. Carol turns to see Jonathan, drunk, walk into the kitchen, carrying a nearly empty bottle of whisky. He goes over to Ella but she starts crying. Carol tries to pull him away from her but he pushes her backwards. She stumbles up against a wall and knocks the radio so it stops playing. There is a moment of stillness.

Jack's race car drives up against Jonathan's feet. He scoops it up, and in a flash of temper, throws it against the wall. He glances at Jack and Ella and then turns to leave. The front door slams behind him, the car starts and reverses rapidly out of the driveway.

Jack looks over at his race car. It is smashed to pieces.

INT. FUNCTION ROOM – PRESENT DAY, EARLY EVENING

The room is emptying – only Ella, Carol, Jean and Billy remain. Billy shakes hands with the staff, thanking them for their service. Jack follows Carol, who has Ella asleep in her arms, out of the room. They walk from the hotel and into the descending darkness of outside.

INT. HALLWAY/KITCHEN – LATER

Jean and Billy hug Carol goodbye. Jack watches from the kitchen table. Carol shuts the door behind her parents and immediately goes through into the living room.

Jack is left alone in the kitchen.

INT. JACK'S BEDROOM – NIGHT

Jack wakes up. He can hear Carol faintly crying downstairs.

INT. LIVING ROOM – NIGHT

Carol is sitting on the sofa, covered in a blanket. She is bathed in a blue glow from the TV. Jack enters and crawls under the blanket with her. They fall asleep.

INT. JACK'S BEDROOM – NIGHT

The single lamp on Jack's desk is on. It is shining on the blue race car, which has been glued back together by Jack. It isn't perfect, but it will race again.

The lamp is switched off.

FADE OUT.

Edward Dyer began life in Coventry, where he used writing as one of many outlets for his creativity. He believes that you should only do what you find challenging. So, if given the chance, his next project would be to build a tree house.

MARIAMA IVES-MOIBA

Three Bridesmaids, a Snickers and a Bathtub

The inside of a Hummer. Two bridesmaids, NICOLE (27) *and* ANGIE (27), *wear fluorescent pink dresses with excessive embroidery and flowers.* REBECCA (28), *in a halter neck version, climbs into the vehicle. Their* DRIVER *sits in front, he reads a newspaper.*

REBECCA: (*Emotional*) She's gone.
ANGIE: (*Laughs*) Yeah, sure.
NICOLE: What do you mean, she's gone?
REBECCA: I looked everywhere!
ANGIE: You're joking, right?
NICOLE: Becky, look at me, where's she gone?
ANGIE: (*To* NICOLE) Becky knows where she's gone.
REBECCA: (*To* ANGIE) If I knew, I would say where she'd gone! You know how people say, 'oh she's gone to the shops' or 'she's gone home', or 'she's gone to take a fucking bath', but what you're failing to understand is that I don't know where she's gone, hence why I said, she's gone!

ANGIE *wipes* REBECCA's *spit from her face.* NICOLE *kisses her teeth.*

NICOLE: What are we gonna tell Jamie?
REBECCA: Nobody's going to tell Jamie anything, because we are going to find her.
NICOLE: How? You said you looked everywhere.
REBECCA: I am not going down as the maid of honour who lost her bride, OK?

NICOLE: Oh for flip sake, nobody cares that you are the maid of honour!
REBECCA: You so do care! You can't stand not being in control. Well, I'm sorry, Nic, but it's my time to shine.
ANGIE: Are you a fucking star?
NICOLE: You're right, Becky, you're in charge and this is your 'moment to shine'. The fact that you lost the bride might dampen your shine a bit, but…
REBECCA: Oh my God, everyone's going to blame meeee!
ANGIE: We could just call her?

Beat.

REBECCA: Yes! Of course! Does she have her phone?
ANGIE: I dunno.
REBECCA: (*Dangerous*) Then why say we should call her?

ANGIE *ignores* REBECCA, *takes her phone out of her clutch bag and dials. The bride's phone rings inside the Hummer.* REBECCA *and* NICOLE *sigh.* ANGIE *listens intently. She awkwardly climbs over them in the cramped space.*

NICOLE: Angie, what the—
REBECCA: Sit down!

ANGIE *triumphantly pulls the missing phone from between the seats. She answers it.*

ANGIE: *(Into phone)* Hello?

REBECCA *and* NICOLE *stare at* ANGIE *in disbelief. She's answering her own phone call.*

ANGIE: (*Laughs*) Oh yeah!

ANGIE *hangs up and places both phones in her lap.*

ANGIE: So, what's plan B?
NICOLE: OK, let's think, where would you go, if you were a bride doing a runner?
REBECCA: Not where a bride would go, where Shanice would go.

They think hard. NICOLE *yanks up the top of her dress.* REBECCA *looks out the window.* ANGIE *stares up at the ceiling.*

ANGIE: I know!
NICOLE & REBECCA: Where?
ANGIE: No, no, she probably wouldn't go there! We could go, just to check, I mean, it's good to be thorough, right?

NICOLE *and* REBECCA *stare at* ANGIE, *confused.*

ANGIE: (*Continues*) That male strip joint up in Soho, I mean, that was a great hen night. I think we learnt a lot… about ourselves… and the bendiness of men.
REBECCA: Are you even taken this seriously?
ANGIE: I'm just trying to lighten the mood! It's Shanice's wedding day, it's a big day, it's a big fucking day. Shit, we've lost the bride!
REBECCA: I can't believe this is happening, oh my God, I can't breathe, I can't breathe.
ANGIE: Woah, just relax! We've already lost the bride, we don't need a dead bridesmaid.
REBECCA: Oh my God, oh… my God.
NICOLE: Becky, calm down. I think you two should go out there and look for her.
ANGIE: Why us?
NICOLE: I'll stay in case she comes back.
ANGIE: You go, I'll stay.
NICOLE: Why you?
ANGIE: If she sees me, I'll have a calming effect on her.
REBECCA: What the—?
ANGIE: I just have that effect on people! I mean, are you stressed right now?
REBECCA: Yes, of course I am, we've lost the fucking bride!
ANGIE: Yeah, see, I'm not stressed and I think this is kinda the aura which would be good for her…
NICOLE: There's no way I am traipsing up and down that high street in these heels and this hideous dress.

NICOLE *yanks up the top of her dress, one of the flowers fall off.* REBECCA *smiles.* ANGIE's *mortified.*

ANGIE: What?! We look fabulous!

Beat. They really don't. They look like an explosion in a pink candy floss factory, and far from edible. ANGIE *picks up the fallen flower and proffers it to* NICOLE. NICOLE *gives* ANGIE *the death-stare.*

NICOLE: Angie, I get that you like to like... everything, but this, this goes against everything I believe in.

ANGIE *holds the flower tight, protecting it from this onslaught.*

NICOLE: Like... life. Yes, this, this monstrosity is not life, it's death. I am wearing a hot pink floral garment of death!
ANGIE: Maybe that's the look Shanice was going for. You know, all that not upstaging the bride stuff. Make your bridesmaids look like death!

NICOLE *grabs the flower out of* ANGIE's *hand and rips it in half.* ANGIE *stares at* NICOLE, *horror-struck.*

REBECCA: Hello! We've lost the fucking bride!
NICOLE: Oh yes, Ms Halter Neck! You try mushing these hooters into a strapless corset without looking like you've swallowed a lump.
ANGIE: I'm gonna call you Lumpy!

NICOLE *fumes.*

ANGIE: Or maybe I won't.

REBECCA *starts to cry.*

Beat.

NICOLE: Are you crying?
REBECCA: (*Wails*) I'm not crying, I'm... just... upseeettt!
ANGIE: Aww, don't cry Becky.
REBECCA: (*Shouts*) I'm not crying!
ANGIE: All right. Jees! (*Beat*) Cry baby.

REBECCA *dives at* ANGIE. NICOLE *jumps in between them.*

NICOLE: Becky, stop it! We're sorry, aren't we Ange?
ANGIE: (*Looks out the window*) It's raining.

REBECCA *and* NICOLE *both peer out of the window. It's chucking it down.*

ANGIE: She must be getting soaked. I'm definitely not going out. Me and rain do not work.
NICOLE: Who does?
ANGIE: Some people look good wet. I look good dry, I'm a good-looking dry person.
REBECCA: Nicole knows all about being wet at inappropriate times.
NICOLE: Do you have to bring that up? Like, always?
REBECCA: I never bring it up!
ANGIE: You kinda do bring it up.
REBECCA: I only bring it up when it's relevant.
NICOLE: How's it relevant?
ANGIE: It really isn't relevant.
REBECCA: Angie, I swear to God.
NICOLE: You bring it up every time you want to make me feel guilty!
REBECCA: If you feel guilty, then that's because you did something wrong!
NICOLE: The juice spilt.
ANGIE: The juice didn't spill.

NICOLE *fumes right up into* ANGIE's *face.*

REBECCA: She's right, Nic, the juice didn't spill. You literally poured it all over yourself so that Craig would be transfixed by your tits through that flimsy-arse blouse.

Still nose-to-nose with the fuming NICOLE, ANGIE *blinks.*

ANGIE: (*Small voice*) They are pretty nice tits.
NICOLE: Thank you.

Mollified, she lets ANGIE *go.*

REBECCA: This is typical, you two always gang up on me.
NICOLE: Oh, please!
REBECCA: I guess you both think it's my fault that Shanice has bolted?
NICOLE: It was your idea to list all of Jamie's faults right before the wedding.
REBECCA: I, I thought it would be fun, to, to list all the things he did that annoyed her and we would laugh, and, and it wouldn't matter because despite those things, despite all of those things, she still loved him.
NICOLE: That's not fun.
ANGIE: Do you know the meaning of fun?
REBECCA: I've always been told I'm fun.
NICOLE: Oh, Gawd…
REBECCA: Remember that time we went to that restaurant and I asked the cute waiter guy for some tap water and he said it would have to be bottled because the taps weren't working? I said… wait what did I say… aah that's it, I said, maybe you better let me back there, so I can loosen the tap and let it, free flowly, flowly flee, flee flow, no—

ANGIE *howls at this.*

REBECCA: See! That was funny, I'm funny, get rid of the N,Y, and I'm fun!
NICOLE: She's laughing at your inability to say flow freely, you're not funny, you're just stupid.

Beat.

REBECCA: I'm gonna give you a moment to retract that statement.

NICOLE and REBECCA *flex their manicures, ready for combat.*
SHANICE's *phone rings.* NICOLE *and* REBECCA *react too slowly,* ANGIE *picks up.*

ANGIE: (*Into phone*) Hello?

ANGIE *rips the phone from her ear and covers it with her hand.*

ANGIE: It's Jamie.
NICOLE: Noooo!
REBECCA: Why did you pick up?

NICOLE: No, no, no, no!
REBECCA: Why, why?
ANGIE: (*Into phone, falsely cheerful*) Hello Jamie, how are you on this fine day? Yes, we're all here, no one's run away, every single person is still with us. Well, it was great speaking to you and we will see you at the wedding, OK then, bye. (*Hangs up, normal voice*) There, done.

A fuming REBECCA and NICOLE are about to hurl themselves upon ANGIE. The phone rings again, they all stare at it. ANGIE opens the window and chucks the phone out of the car. REBECCA and NICOLE stare at her, horror-struck. ANGIE chuckles with relief.

ANGIE: Close one.

The phone rings from outside the Hummer. ANGIE closes the window. Silence. REBECCA and NICOLE take a moment to react.

ANGIE: (*Light dawning*) We're all so stupid!

REBECCA leans forward to attack ANGIE, NICOLE holds her back.

REBECCA: Let me go!

ANGIE: (*Bangs on the window separating them from the driver*) Driver, driver!

He opens the window.

DRIVER: Are you ladies ready to go?
ANGIE: We're sort of in a pickle. You see, we've lost the bride.
DRIVER: Huh?
ANGIE: She got out for a breath of fresh air, never came back.
DRIVER: You lost the bride?
NICOLE: Technically, she ran away.
DRIVER: What sort of bridesmaids can't keep hold of the bride?

Three very, very pissed-off ladies.

REBECCA: Look, buddy, we didn't ask for the lowdown on what bridesmaids should or shouldn't do, so when Angie knocked on your shitty-arse window and said 'driver', I'm sure you can guess what she wanted you to do!

Silence. The DRIVER *runs through the options in his head.*

ALL: (*Screech*) Drive!
DRIVER: To the church?
REBECCA: No, not to the church, we don't have a bride, you imbecile!
DRIVER: Hey, I'm just doing my job, I could kick you guys out right now…

Three very, very pissed-off ladies giving him the evil eye.

DRIVER: But… I won't… because… because, I'm a gentleman.
REBECCA: Oh, he's a gentleman, I'm so glad we got lucky.
DRIVER: Where am I driving to?
ANGIE: Just around the area, she has to be here somewhere.
NICOLE: What if we don't find her?
REBECCA: Well, we will, because it's not like she hid a passport and suitcase up her dress and is going through luggage check at Heathrow fucking Airport right now!
NICOLE: You know, sometimes you don't have to answer. Sometimes a question can just be left out there. You know?

Silence. They all watch it, out there – floating in mid-air.

NICOLE: Yeah, just like that.
REBECCA: You do look like a mush of lumps.

NICOLE's *blindsided.*

NICOLE: Sorry?
REBECCA: I said, you do… look like… a mush of lumps.

NICOLE *dives at* REBECCA *and rips the top of her halter neck dress.*

DRIVER: Oh, yeah!

REBECCA *and* NICOLE *slap at each other,* ANGIE *jumps in and wrestles them both down on the back seat. They kick and slap and scream. The car door opens, and* SHANICE *enters the Hummer. The girls freeze.* SHANICE *puts down her umbrella and sits, fluffing out her dress.*

REBECCA: Shanice, where the hell have you been?
SHANICE: I went to the shop for a Snickers, walked home and sat and ate it in the bathtub. (*Beat*) Needed some time to think. Plus Jamie's allergic to nuts, (*Starts to cry*) so that was probably my last Snick… (*Howls*)

They all crowd around and comfort her.

ANGIE: You can come round mine anytime for a Snickers.
SHANICE: (*Continues to howl*) Thank yooouuu.
DRIVER: So… drive?

Mariama Ives-Moiba is of mixed heritage – British and Sierra Leonean. She won the Trinity International Playwriting Competition with her play *A Concrete Jungle Full of Wild Cars* in 2012, which was taken to the Edinburgh Fringe Festival in 2013. She enjoys writing for theatre, but is expanding into different media.

TOM LASHLEY

Time's Up

FADE IN:

EXT. SUBURBAN STREET. NORTH CORNWALL – DAY

Refracted sunrays cast spotlights on the honey-coloured leaves that pepper the suburban pavement. Half-naked trees loom over long driveways that wind their way to large houses, each a carbon copy of its neighbour.

The neighbourhood is small, containing around fifteen houses in total and with lots of space in between.

One house has a magnolia tree in the front garden – large, blowsy, purple flower buds ready to burst. The house has the same quality; a little over the top. Paintwork a shade too blue. Two carriage-lamps on either side of the front door. Through the bay window, swagged curtains festoon the glass.

This is Dale's house.

INT. DALE'S HOUSE. LIVING ROOM – SAME

Beethoven's *Moonlight Sonata* reverberates through the house. The sound system from which it is playing seems too modern for the CD of choice.

We pan around the ostentatiously-decorated living room. Past the over-crowded wall of replica paintings – Van Gogh's *Sunflowers*, Rembrandt's *Saint Bartholomew*. Past the purple grand piano that has clearly never been touched, and the armchair too big for anything human to sit in comfortably.

A wiry-framed boy is sitting on the sofa. This is DALE, 15. Acne and adolescent wear and tear have taken their toll on his skin. He is dressed in cargo shorts and a baggy T-shirt. He looks out of place in the setting.

His eyes are transfixed on the muted television, his ears on the music.

He is watching cartoons, Wile E Coyote and The Road Runner fight on screen. Wile E Coyote throws a lightning bolt at The Road Runner, who turns and runs.

The doorbell rings, but it is only just audible above Beethoven's overtures.

Dale stands and edges to the hallway, not taking his eyes off the screen. The lightning bolt is chasing The Road Runner around mountains, through tunnels—

The doorbell rings again.

INT. DALE'S HOUSE. HALLWAY – CONTINUOUS

Dale opens the door.

KYNA, 16, is on the doorstep. She is taller than Dale, has unkempt, unwashed hair, and is wearing commando-style trousers, a muddied vest top, and a torn trench coat. A bulging backpack pulls at her shoulders. All she's missing is war paint on her face. She stoops to kiss Dale on his cheek.

INT. DALE'S HOUSE. LIVING ROOM – CONTINUOUS

Kyna strides in, looks to the television where the lightning bolt is now attacking Wile E Coyote.

She turns it off, puts her backpack down and opens it. She hands Dale a large coat and trousers similar to hers. He strips and puts them on.

Kyna rummages through the bag. Metal clunks together as she does so.

Dale has put one of his arms through the wrong sleeve of his coat. Kyna untangles him and straightens it out.

Kyna goes into her bag and pulls out a camera. She snaps a picture of Dale, who looks down at his feet.

INT. KYNA'S CAR – LATER

A beat-up, rusting Fiesta. The inside is full of old fast-food boxes and drinks bottles that rattle around the floor.

On the windscreen is a large sticker that reads 'The British Association for Shooting and Conservation', and another that says 'Game is for playing'.

Kyna drives, Dale is in the passenger seat. The radio is on.

A current chart pop song comes on, Kyna turns it over to a classical music station.

The car rumbles on to the sounds of Schubert. Every bump feels like the car is going to fall apart.

They stop at a zebra crossing to let a MAN cross. He holds his hand up to say 'thank you,' but as he gets to the other side does a double take and stares at Kyna – she is clearly underage. Kyna accelerates off before he has time to say anything.

Dale inhales heavily. Holds it. Exhales. Kyna glances at him, touches his knee. He half-smiles at her, all he can muster.

Dale's breathing quickens. He shuts his eyes, strains, trying to calm his breathing. It doesn't work.

He looks out the window, attempting to hide it from Kyna.

But it is too late, she's noticed.

His breaths are getting shorter.

Kyna reaches to the backseat, sifts through her bag. She passes Dale his inhaler. He sucks on it, throws his head back, and breathes in and out.

Dale winds down the window and throws his inhaler out. He rests his head back and shuts his eyes.

EXT. CAR PARK – LATER

An expansive car park next to a field that stretches for miles. There are many spaces, but Kyna has parked as far back as she can.

Kyna gets out of the car with the backpack and opens the boot. Dale takes his time, as though getting out of the car requires all his body strength.

When he gets to the boot, he peers in. He looks to Kyna, back to the contents. A look of dread crosses his face, but he gets rid of it before Kyna notices.

Kyna pulls out large, thick chains, followed by industrial-sized padlocks. She hands them to Dale, who almost buckles under the weight.

From the boot, Kyna takes out a small box. It is a brand new 'Go Pro' – a small video camera to attach to one's head.

She smiles at Dale. He ignores her.

Kyna opens the box and straps the 'Go Pro' around Dale's forehead. She turns it on. She gets out another 'Go Pro' and puts it on.

Dale and Kyna look back into the boot. She reaches in with both hands.

EXT. FIELD – LATER

Kyna strides ahead of Dale across the field next to the car park, both have their coats done up. Kyna keeps having to hoist her backpack up.

Kyna looks back to Dale, and then forwards. Dale follows her gaze.

They are heading, inexorably, towards a school.

EXT. SCHOOL. CAFETERIA – LATER

Outside a set of double doors. Paint has crumbled off, the beginnings of rust are visible around the edges of windows. Dale has a set of chains draped around his shoulders like a scarf. He looks around. Deserted.

Dale peers through the window. Inside is a cafeteria that is currently empty. In the kitchen at the back steam is rising as there is cooking in progress.

Dale takes the chains from his shoulders and wraps them round the door handles. He crops it a few times so it is tight. He pulls the door and it hardly budges. He takes a padlock out of his pocket and clamps it shut through the chains.

EXT. SCHOOL. BACK DOORS – SAME

Another set of doors. Kyna wraps her chains around the door handles without hesitation. She padlocks them and smiles.

EXT. SCHOOL. ENTRANCE – LATER

Both Dale and Kyna are now sat at a small wooden picnic table. The furniture you only ever see in schools. It is by the school's main entrance, the only door they have not locked shut.

Dale is shivering, but it is not cold. Kyna puts her hands over his. She tries to look into his eyes but his gaze is fixed on the table.

A ladybird lands in front of him. Its red and black spots appear sharp against the dull brown of the table.
Dale takes his hands from Kyna's and puts his finger in front of the ladybird.

It turns away, looking for an escape route. Dale uses another finger to block its path. And another.

Eventually it crawls onto his finger. He lifts his finger close to his eye, as if he were trying to count the exact number of spots on its back.

The ladybird crawls up, down, and around his finger. He holds out another, and another, and lets it crawl all over his hand.

He places his finger slowly, carefully, next to the table surface. The ladybird crawls off.

Kyna squashes the ladybird with her thumb.

Finally, Dale looks into her eyes.

Kyna grabs Dale's wrist and looks at his watch. It is 12:29pm.

She stands and reaches into her backpack.

She pulls out a Glock pistol. And with it, a book. She places the gun on the table, the book over it, and pushes it over to Dale.

He stares at the book – a maths workbook. He opens the cover and sees handwritten: Dale Meadows. Year 8. Class 8A.

Dale flicks to different pages, all of which are covered in green ticks and comments such as 'Great work,' 'Well done,' and a sticker that reads 'You're a star!'

Kyna shuts the book.

The lunch bell sounds from inside the school.

Kyna takes off her coat to reveal a hunting rifle strapped to her back. She swings it round, ready.

The lunch bell stops. School children's excitable clamour becomes audible.

Dale does not move.

Kyna throws the book to one side. She tries to push the pistol into Dale's hands. They stay clamped shut. As clamped as the school's doors.

> KYNA
>
> Take it.

Kyna stands back, staring at Dale.

Dale continues to look at the table, not moving an inch.

She SHOOTS Dale in the head with the pistol.

For a split second, it seems as though Kyna is going to shed a tear. But she closes her eyes and takes a deep breath, composing herself.

Kyna opens her eyes and makes her way to the entrance.

She opens the doors and enters.

They swing closed, the chains rattle as she wraps the door handles and padlocks from the inside.

Her footsteps fade as she walks away, into the school.

FADE OUT.

Tom Lashley is a scriptwriter, with the goal to write for the screen. Since starting his Master's degree, however, he has enjoyed exploring creative ideas through stage and radio plays, as well as advancing his screenwriting. Now, he does not want to limit himself to just one medium, and will aim to utilise all media for his future writing.

MARK PROBERT

Bairstow-Minghella

A short comedy for the stage.

Cast

Charlotte (23) Intern

Jenny (22) Intern

Oz (48) Accounts Director

The action takes place in a small meeting room in the offices of advertising, PR and marketing company, Bairstow-Minghella.

Lights up to reveal CHARLOTTE & JENNY sitting at a table c/s. There is a flip chart and a chair s/r. They have been there for some time. Jenny, relentlessly perky, has a pad and paper ready and is busying herself retouching her make-up. Charlotte, more cynical and world-weary, is unenthusiastically scrolling through her phone. Distracted by Jenny's preening, she stares at her. Jenny notices her staring, flashes her a smile and goes back to primping. Charlotte shakes her head, slumps forward and bangs her head on the desk with bored frustration. After a time, OZ bursts in s/l and both girls jump up.

OZ Ah, this is where you two are hiding. Right, well, come on. Time and tide wait for no man.

He strides over to the flip chart: the girls gather up their stuff and move towards the door.

OZ   Where are you going?

CHARLOTTE   Um, well we thought—

OZ   Off for a tea break already, ladies? There's work to be done.

The girls retake their seats, Charlotte with a sigh.

OZ   We can have a cuppa and a celebratory custard cream when we've cracked this and not before. Right, you. *(Indicating Charlotte)* What's your name? Paula, any ideas.

CHARLOTTE   Um, er, sorry, it's—

OZ   Never apologise. Never explain.

CHARLOTTE   Right. But my name—

OZ   What's wrong with it?

CHARLOTTE   Nothing. But you called me Paula.

OZ   And?

CHARLOTTE   That's not my name. I'm Charlotte.

OZ   Are you sure?

CHARLOTTE   Well, yes, unless my parents have been lying to me all these years.

OZ   Because you look like a Paula.

CHARLOTTE   Er.

Charlotte looks lost. Jenny shoots up her hand.

OZ   Yes?

JENNY   You can call me 'Paula' if you like, Mr Minghella.

OZ   That won't be necessary. I know your name. It's Ginny, isn't it?

JENNY   *(Nodding enthusiastically)* That's right, Mr Minghella.

Charlotte frowns.

OZ   Please, call me Oz. Everybody does. Short for Osberto. Besides, you look nothing like Paula.

Oz turns to the flipchart and writes 'Staybright' in large letters.

CHARLOTTE *(Whispering)* I thought your name was *Jenny* not *Ginny*.

Jenny furiously motions for her to keep quiet.

OZ   Right. 'Staybright'. You. *(Indicating Jenny)* Thoughts.

JENNY   Um.

OZ   Too slow. Time is money. What about you? *(Indicating Charlotte)*

CHARLOTTE What about Staybright?

OZ   'What about Staybright?'!

CHARLOTTE I thought that was all signed off.

OZ   Well, you thought wrong, Not-Paula. We've got the clients upstairs and they're none too happy. We need a new strapline pronto. So do something to justify your wages and get with the programme!

CHARLOTTE We don't get wages.

OZ   What?

CHARLOTTE   You don't pay us. We're interns.

OZ   Explain it to her, somebody.

JENNY   As interns, while we are not actually remunerated in monetary terms, we are paid in kind. The name of Bairstow-Minghella on our CVs and a favourable reference will guarantee us a position in any advertising, marketing or public relations company in the world we would wish to apply to.

OZ   Correct!

CHARLOTTE   *(Under her breath)* Some little swot's done their homework.

OZ   So, while there's no cash, there is cachet.

CHARLOTTE   OK, well, in that case give me a job.

OZ   What?

CHARLOTTE   If the name Bairstow-Mingella guarantees me a job in any advertising, marketing or PR company in the world and this is indeed an advertising, marketing and PR company, give me a job. A proper job. For real money.

OZ   *(Suppressing his annoyance)* I suppose you think you're very clever.

CHARLOTTE   I got a first at Oxford which tends to imply something of the sort.

OZ   Well, Miss Magna Cum Laude, as Geraldine has pointed out, any appointment would also be dependent on a favourable reference, a favourable reference from me:

which at the moment is a dim and distant dream. Right, so back to the matter in hand. Staybright. You have thirty seconds to brainstorm as many straplines as you can. *(Using his phone as a stopwatch.)* On your marks, get set, go!

Jenny starts writing furiously. Charlotte has no paper or pen. She tries to attract Jenny's attention by tugging her sleeve. Jenny shrugs her off. Charlotte hisses at her: Jenny covers her ears.

OZ	*(Staring at his watch)* Ten seconds.

CHARLOTTE	*(In an urgent whisper)* I haven't got a pen. *(Jenny ignores her. She leans closer.)* Lend me some paper. *(Jenny shuffles away.)*

OZ	I hear whispering: I don't hear scribbling. Twenty seconds.

Charlotte makes a grab for some paper. Jenny's hand immediately shoots up.

JENNY	Mr Minghella.

OZ	*(Without looking up)* What is it, Jilly?

JENNY	Charlotte's copying.

OZ	What?

CHARLOTTE	No, I'm not.

OZ	Well, what are you doing all over her side of the desk then?

CHARLOTTE	I wanted to borrow a pen and paper.

OZ	Haven't you got your own?

CHARLOTTE	No.

OZ   Why not?

CHARLOTTE   I wasn't told I'd need any.

OZ   Gerry managed to bring some.

Jenny looks smug.

CHARLOTTE   I wasn't told anything except to come here and wait for you. And that was forty-five minutes ago.

OZ   Oh, so it's my fault.

CHARLOTTE   What?

OZ   I'm obviously to blame for not giving you clear instructions and keeping you waiting, am I?

CHARLOTTE   That's not what I said.

OZ   Well, I'll have you know, young lady, that I was in Meeting Room One, *Meeting Room One*, with the head honcho from Staybright trying to persuade him to keep their account with us. I was working hard to ensure we all have a future. What were you doing might I ask?

CHARLOTTE   Nothing.

OZ   Precisely!

CHARLOTTE   I wasn't told to do anything.

OZ   Well, I'm telling you now. We have the time it takes him to drink a skinny latte to come up with a slogan for Staybright or we're all for the high jump. *(To Jenny)* Right, what have you got?

JENNY   *(Standing)* Well, it's still work in progress.

OZ   Not expecting Sistine Chapel straight off.

JENNY   But I thought, 'Staybright'.

There is a pause while the others wait for more. Jenny sits looking pleased with herself.

OZ   Right.

CHARLOTTE   Is that it?

JENNY   It's short and to the point.

CHARLOTTE   But all you've done is restate the product's name.

JENNY   I said it wasn't finished.

CHARLOTTE   It's not even started.

JENNY   Well, it's more than you've written.

CHARLOTTE   I haven't written anything because you wouldn't give me one of your precious pens.

JENNY   It's not my fault you're unprepared.

OZ   Girls, girls, please! That's quite enough of that. *(They fall sulky silent)* Thank you. Now, we're not there yet, Genevieve, but you've made a start. A journey of a thousand miles starts with a single step.

JENNY   *(To Charlotte)* See.

CHARLOTTE   But all she's—

OZ   You've put down a marker in the sand and out of such small acorns who knows what mighty oak trees will grow. Not the finished article yet but A* for effort.

JENNY	Thank you, sir.
OZ	And as you rightly point out, where's Not-Paula's contribution, eh?
JENNY	*(Giggling)* 'Not-Paula.'
CHARLOTTE	*(Mumbling)* The dog ate it.
OZ	What?
CHARLOTTE	Just give me a moment.
OZ	We're waiting.
CHARLOTTE	Um... How about, er...
OZ	It's your time you're wasting.
CHARLOTTE	'Stay white, stay light with Staybright.'

Pause.

OZ	Rubbish.
JENNY	I agree.
CHARLOTTE	What!?
OZ	Total garbage.
CHARLOTTE	It's better than hers.
OZ	*(Hushing her)* Tut-tut. Wait... wait a moment... I'm getting something. I'm getting something. Ah! Got it! 'Stay white, stay light, Staybright!'
JENNY	*(Clapping)* Oh, well done, sir!

CHARLOTTE   But that's what I said!

OZ   No, you didn't!

CHARLOTTE   Yes, I did!

OZ   You said nothing of the sort.

CHARLOTTE   I did. That's precisely what I said.

OZ   Are you arguing with me, young lady?

CHARLOTTE   Well—

OZ   You said, 'Stay white, stay light *with* Staybright.' My strapline used no such conjunction and is therefore altogether punchier and more successful.

CHARLOTTE   'With' is a preposition not a conjunction.

OZ   It's one bloody word too many is what it is. How dare you try to take credit for my creativity?

JENNY   Yeah, and I even gave you 'Staybright'.

CHARLOTTE   No you didn't; that's the name of the bloody product!

OZ   Don't use such language in front of me. Now write out a hundred times. 'I must not steal other people's work and pass it off as my own.' Well? Get on with it.

CHARLOTTE   I would if I had a pen and paper.

JENNY   Here, you can borrow mine.

OZ   Thank you, Jezebel.

JENNY   And would you like an apple, sir?

OZ   Oh, er, how very kind, Jocasta. One of my five a day, eh? I'll save it for later if you don't mind.

Jenny sticks out her tongue at Charlotte.

CHARLOTTE   *(Under her breath)* Teacher's pet.

JENNY   *(Under her breath)* Thicko.

CHARLOTTE   *(Under her breath)* Creep.

JENNY   *(Under her breath)* Smelly.

CHARLOTTE   *(Under her breath)* Arse-licker.

JENNY   *(Putting up her hand)* Sir, Not-Paula swore.

CHARLOTTE   She started it. She stuck her tongue out.

OZ   My star pupil? She wouldn't dream of doing such a thing. Right, Not-Paula, I've just about had enough of you today. You can just jolly well sit there quietly with your hands on your head. Julia, you can get a book out and do some private reading.

JENNY   Oh, goody.

Jenny gets a copy of Black Beauty *out and starts to read. Oz sits on the chair s/r and lights his pipe.*

CHARLOTTE   *(Under her breath)* Just you wait till break time.

They sit in silence for some time. Smoke begins to drift on to stage. Charlotte is the first to notice it.

CHARLOTTE   Er…

OZ   Little girls should be seen and not heard.

Charlotte tries to attract Jenny's attention who thinks it's part of the threatened assault and takes out a pair of compasses to defend herself. Jenny eventually notices the smoke.

JENNY   Er, Mr Minghella.

OZ   Yes, Jocelyn.

JENNY   There's smoke.

OZ   Yes, I know: it's just my pipe. Back to work.

The girls are silently panicking. A fire alarm sounds. The girls are wide-eyed with fear. After a moment's hesitation, they get up.

OZ   The bell is a signal for me not for you.

OZ indicates they should sit down. Confused and conflicted, the girls retake their places. Smoke fills the stage. The girls begin to choke. We have all the Time in the World *by Louis Armstrong plays as the lights fade.*

Mark Probert graduated from Exeter with a BA in Drama back in the eighties. He worked in the professional theatre as a performer and as a technician for several years before taking a PGCE at The Central School of Speech and Drama. He has been a drama teacher in schools for the past fifteen years, writing and devising many shows, often with the collaboration of pupils.

MICHELLE SEWELL

The Tinder Game

The Tinder Game is a verbatim play which takes real conversations from the dating app, Tinder, and mixes them with interviews of people's thoughts and experiences of the game.

Cast of Characters

JAMES: 24, MALE. About James: Me – ambitious, adventurous, caring, 5'7".

LIZ: 24, FEMALE. About Liz: writer, ambitious, foreign.

CHRISSY: 23, FEMALE. About Chrissy: I'm 5'9" since everyone is putting their height. Stalk me here Chrissy_Lord.

ABI: 29, MALE. About Abi: Norwich, Bearded and single.

Writer's Note:

The stage is separated into four glass boxes which contain the worlds of CHRISSY, LIZ, JAMES and ABI. They should be distinctly different worlds. When in the Tinder World, they are lit in red.

A / means a character interrupts.

Spelling and grammar errors and emoticons indicate messaging and speech patterns and behaviours of characters. The words do not need to be said how they are written, but can be.

If a character's name appears multiple times in consecutive order, they are sending multiple messages.

The TINDER (VO) is a recorded voice. It can be any age or gender.

ONE

LIZ's box is lit. She stands. As Tinder loads, the loading sign washes over her.

TINDER (VO) *begins to speak.*
Tinder. 17 Plus.

Anonymously 'Like' or 'Pass' on pictures of people Tinder suggests in your area.

A picture of a random, KALEM, washes over her.

Not Interested? A swipe-left on a picture indicates you're not interested and they're gone.

A picture of JAMES washes over her capsule.

Like? A swipe-right on a picture indicates you like James. Mutual swipe-rights are informed of their match and then given the ability to contact each other.

Rule One. Be good looking.

Rule Two. Never message immediately after a match. Always wait at least one to two hours.

Rule Three. Do not fall in love.

Rule Four. Don't drink and Tinder.

Rule Five. Don't get too scroll-happy, you may accidentally say 'no' to a 'yes'. There are absolutely no do-overs in the Tinder World.

Welcome to Tinder!

> *Liz stands, curious, as photos of men and women scroll over her.*

LIZ
No. No. No. Definitely not. Ew… no no… oh hello!…

TWO

> *In Tinder World. The happy beeping and vibrating noise of Tinder. Lights up on everyone. CHRISSY and LIZ standing, JAMES leaning, ABI sitting.*

TINDER (VO)
Congratulations! You have a new match! Message or Keep Playing?

> *Silence.*

JAMES
Hey

LIZ
Hey

CHRISSY
Hiya

ABI
Hoya

CHRISSY
Morning!

ABI
So you're less than a kilometre away… Whereabouts would that be?

JAMES
Hi, how/ are you? :)

CHRISSY
Hey I'm good!/ How are you?

ABI
Hiya what's/ cracking?

CHRISSY
Hi Liz,/ thanks for swiping right. Sweet pics, are you a student? X

JAMES
Hey Chrissy, I'm James/ how are you

LIZ
Hey! Cute dog

CHRISSY
Heya!/ Good weekend? X

ABI
Hel/loo

JAMES
Hey :D How's you?

ABI
If you had to be mauled to death by an animal what would be the worst way to go

LIZ giggles.

CHRISSY
Based on your pics you have quite a leap, lol.

JAMES
I was really hoping you'd match with me.

ABI
I'd say orca, because they don't just kill you, they play with you first.

LIZ crosses her arms.

CHRISSY
Bonsoir! Thanks for the swipy-ness, it's warmed me up a little as I'm stuck in the cold waiting for a/ bus this evening, brr! X

JAMES
I really liked your profile.

LIZ
Thanks./ How are you?

ABI
I am/ good.

LIZ
Do you come here often??

CHRISSY
Not particularly/ no, do you?

LIZ
Nice Selfie!

ABI stands.

JAMES
Blue penguins.

Sorry, just wanted something to break the ice

CHRISSY giggles and lies down.

LIZ
So what do you do?

JAMES
I live an exciting life and work in retail!/ How about yourself?

CHRISSY
You want to break ice with penguins??? Surely a polar bear is/ more fitting!

LIZ
I'm a student.

JAMES laughs

ABI
You should see a doctor, because you're lacking vitamin me! :p

JAMES
Ha

CHRISSY
Haha, it took me a minute to realise that wasn't a real question, but a classic pick-up line… haha derp

LIZ
Ah cool!/ Do you enjoy working in retail?

CHRISSY
I'm in my bed, I'm a little bad.

CHRISSY touches herself. ABI touches himself. JAMES leans forward.

LIZ
Do you come here often?

ABI
>   Only when nature calls…
>
>   Wanna see how quick I can comb my hair?
>
>   *ABI licks his lips.*

JAMES
>   Did you have/ a good weekend?

CHRISSY
>   Couldn't sleep at all last night

ABI
>   …is this love?

THREE

Not in Tinder World. Spotlight on JAMES.

JAMES
>   So about two years back I was due to meet (yet another) Tinder date. Picnic on the beach. Get her near *me* so I don't have to travel. But… so then she texts me to challenge me to a picnic-off. She makes the sweet and me the savoury.
>
>   Hello, that's different! GAME ON! Spend hours preparing a halloumi and lemon salad! I'll be damned if I am letting her win.
>
>   So I get to this gazebo, early. And I'm standing alone with a picnic looking like a flustered, stood-up, slightly pathetic loner.
>
>   The 10 minutes it took her to arrive felt like an hour. It was well played.
>
>   We dated for a year after that. She kept saying 'how can this be a real thing? We met on Tinder.'… She was the greatest love I've ever known.

FOUR

In Tinder World. Lights up on each box. JAMES sits, CHRISSY leans, LIZ and ABI stand.

JAMES
Hey, nice to match you. Soo guess you've read my profile? :)

LIZ
So what are you on/ Tinder for?

CHRISSY
I did, just now. As a writing student, I felt tempted to advise you to rephrase a bit, but that's just my tendency to meddle.

JAMES
No please meddle.

JAMES
meet new people, see what happens, no real hidden agenda. What are you on here for?

CHRISSY twirls her hair.

ABI
Tbh I'm kinda the live by the gun die by the gun type of guy :p

LIZ and CHRISSY sigh.

LIZ and CHRISSY
Thrilling

ABI slumps.

CHRISSY
Being 'simple and straight to the point' and saying you're just here to hook up is generally less effective than breezily saying you're

looking for something fun and casual towards the end of the profile.

ABI and JAMES
> What about you?

JAMES
> From your profile, it's not clear what you're on here for. However, the description would suggest you're looking for a relationship?

LIZ
> Honestly,/ I'm writing a play at the moment about Tinder.

ABI
> Honestly/ I don't really have any female friends.

JAMES
> Honestly...

CHRISSY
> Honestly... for some no strings attached sex

ABI's box blacks out.

CHRISSY
> However, I prefer to reserve judgement as to whether I'm looking for anything at all – casual or otherwise – until I've met someone in person.

JAMES
> That's cool!

CHRISSY's box blacks out.

LIZ
> Haha! You know you do have the classic picture of – hugging dog photo...

JAMES
> I have so many pictures of me hugging my dog that I've lost count.

LIZ

Hehe!! My dog is sooo far away!!

JAMES chuckles.

JAMES

Where does your dog live?

LIZ pauses.

LIZ

Well I'm from Australia so he's back home in Sydney!!

JAMES slumps.

JAMES

Oh wow! Are you just here studying then or...?

LIZ

Yeah I'm just studying for the year! But I love England and want to stay.

JAMES smiles and tilts his head.

LIZ smiles and catches herself.

FIVE

Not in Tinder World. Spotlight on CHRISSY.

CHRISSY

Let's see so, I already knew a little bit about him because Hannah had already gone on a date with him. All I knew was that he lasted thirty seconds in sex. But! Hannah also told me that he might be my soulmate.

So like I went into it thinking well maybe I can prolong the thirty second thing um… but I'm not, I'm not sleeping with him on the first date. Like I knew that, I knew that right out.

Anyway – so I met him and like… he's nice but he's a little 'take charge.' A little domineering. So we went to this place. The Crypts. He – starts chatting – and he seems kinda cool – like I couldn't hear him that well, but he's drinking… Like a fish.

And – we had this rotate payment. And then here's the thing. Here's the problem with that. He's also interweaving how much he made. I'm like bitch, please, I'm a student.

But I still have this thing in the back of my mind that… even though he's being a little mmmmm… he may be my soulmate.

And then… later in the night he sort, sort of is when he became kind of conservative and kind of crazy… um… and we started talking about… something with politics… and he goes, 'In America, I would have voted for Romney.' And I was like, 'Oh. Shit.'

And he's like 'Financially, I mean, come on, we can't just keep throwing money at poor people… and what it's boiled down to is we're either going to have to keep throwing money at the poor people or let them kind of go off on their own and sink or swim.' And I-ah was-ah mm-like, 'Well, what about the children?' And he said, 'Yeah – that's the hard part.'

Err… And I'm just like. 'Holy. Fuck. What am I doing?' And then he goes straight into stocks. He goes, 'I have stocks in Apple and JP Morgan. So I'm doing very well.'

Meanwhile, we're rotating the drinks.

And I'm just like… mmeeerrhh… And he sees and's like 'Um. I don't kind of see this going anywhere. I kind of just want sex.' And I'm like 'All right. I'm going'.

And that's when I called you.

SIX

In Tinder World. Lights up on ABI and LIZ, standing.

ABI
I'm Abi from Dubai, 29 years old.

LIZ
Oh cool! I'm 24, from Australia.

ABI smiles.

ABI
I like making friends with people to share our experiences.

ABI
Can I have your number and meet later to know each other?

LIZ pauses.

LIZ
Awesome! Do you enjoy your course?

ABI
I'm new in this app.

ABI
It's too hard for us because it's my second language.

ABI
I hate study actually, I like travel and discover the world

LIZ
Yeah! That's awesome. Why England?

ABI presses his hand against the front of the box.

ABI
No reasons for choosing England it's my destiny

ABI
> I would like to invite you to dinner if you have time to know each other

ABI
> Is that too forward?

SEVEN

Not in Tinder World. Spotlight on JAMES.

JAMES
> I'm a single man looking to meet women on Tinder, and I don't just swipe right often, I swipe right always. What's more, I'm usually doing something else while swiping right... watching TV, talking to you... and not even looking at my phone as I do it. It's what men are encouraged to do by how Tinder works and how women use it. Anything else would be a *waste* of our time.

EIGHT

In Tinder World. Lights up on each box. All standing.

LIZ
> OK so I know I probably shouldn't ask cos I said I was only on Tinder for research... but would you want to meet up for coffee or a drink sometime??

JAMES self high-fives.

JAMES
> Yes :) :)

LIZ jumps for joy.

JAMES
If easier I have whatsapp... 07898273922

ABI
Is that your natural hair colour/ by the way?

CHRISSY
Hey, how was/ your day?

ABI
Yeah really/ good thanks.

   LIZ pauses. She considers and is about to reply to JAMES when...

JAMES
Did you watch the rugby? What a game!

   Silence.

JAMES
I'll stop annoying you now but if you fancy getting together you have my number, let me know. Could be fun :)

   LIZ's smile darkens.

   JAMES hits the box.

   ABI sits.

   CHRISSY lies down.

CHRISSY
It's just shopping for sex!

JAMES
Hey! I was thinking I might've got a text from you by now, but obviously something went wrong somewhere.

Scared you off?

Pause.

LIZ
Yes.

JAMES slumps to sit.

JAMES
My bad, what did I do? You seemed chatty and then it just stopped.

JAMES
And also, sorry. I know I went a bit OTT, I wanted to play it cool but I have been having a slightly bad last week or two and wanted something to look forward to.

JAMES
Anyway Liz. Perhaps we could continue from where we left off,/ sometime tomorrow?

CHRISSY
Goodnight.

ABI
It's beaut.

Silence.

Liz's box blacks out.

CHRISSY
??

JAMES
Hey!

ABI
Hey!

JAMES
    Hey?

ABI
    Hey

JAMES
    Boo Liz

CHRISSY
    Hi there x

ABI
    Hey

JAMES
    Hey

The light turns on in LIZ's box.

LIZ
    Hey

Pause.

JAMES
    Ow wow hello! I thought you were gone forever

LIZ
    Just deleted tinder for a bit

JAMES
    Oh so you're back for good?

Silence.

Blackout.

Michelle Sewell is an Australian scriptwriter whose bold, fast-paced pieces examine identity, memory and communication. In 2014, her play *Write Into A War* was produced by Theatre 503. In 2015, her work was featured at the Hotbed and INK Festivals, and she was attached to the Menagerie Theatre Company's Young Writers programme.

JADE TREMBLAY

Too Old For This

Darkness. The SNAP of a lamp being turned on to reveal:

INT. BEDROOM – NIGHT

OLD MAN (81) and OLD WOMAN (77) lie awake in their double bed. They are wearing matching, hideous pajamas. They look up at the ceiling.

> OLD WOMAN
> I think we should get a divorce.

Old Woman keeps her gaze locked on the ceiling. Old Man sneezes – loud, explosive. He takes a moment to compose himself.

> OLD MAN
> What?

> OLD WOMAN
> I said, I think we should get a divorce.

> OLD MAN
> Oh.

Beat. Old Man takes another moment to think this through.

> OLD MAN
> OK.

Old Man turns away from his wife. He attempts to sleep. Old Woman is visibly appalled.

> **OLD WOMAN**
> So that's it? You're just going to accept your fate... like a loser?

> **OLD MAN**
> I'm old.

Stunned silence.

> **OLD WOMAN**
> *I'm* old!

Old Man pushes out a loud, exaggerated sigh for dramatic effect.

> **OLD MAN**
> I guess I feel like I'm too tired for this kind of thing.

> **OLD WOMAN**
> I'm too *old* for this kind of thing.
> (beat)
> Anyways – aren't you at least going to ask me why?

> **OLD MAN**
> OK.

> **OLD WOMAN**
> We don't love each other anymore.

> **OLD MAN**
> (unimpressed)
> Pfft. That's hardly a reason to get divorced. Lots of people don't love each other anymore. No need to get all dramatic about it.

Old Woman scrunches her face together like a pug's. She is choosing her words very, very carefully.

> OLD WOMAN
> It's… your snoring. I can't take it anymore.

> OLD MAN
> What?

> OLD WOMAN
> It's like a symphony in here. Every single night. And not the good kind.

Old Man seems irked by this. He sits up.

> OLD MAN
> What about your many bizarre quirks? You don't hear me complaining.

> OLD WOMAN
> Such as?

> OLD MAN
> You don't like puppies. Everyone likes puppies. If you don't like puppies you are a heartless robot.

> OLD WOMAN
> But I like puppies.

> OLD MAN
> You do not.

> OLD WOMAN
> What are you talking about? I like dogs. That includes baby dogs.

> OLD MAN
> Oh. Why don't we have a dog?

OLD WOMAN
Because you're allergic.

OLD MAN
Am not.

OLD WOMAN
You had an allergy test three years ago. You're allergic to dogs. And cantaloupe.

OLD MAN
(revelatory)
You don't say. Is that why every time I eat cantaloupe, my gums get itchy and I develop a lisp?

Old Woman sighs loudly, trying to one up her husband in volume.

OLD WOMAN
Do you know what I say when Millie, our own *grand-daughter*, asks how we met? I tell her I don't want to talk about it – because that would mean having to think about the day we met.

OLD MAN
Oh. Yikes.

OLD WOMAN
I don't think I ever loved you.

OLD MAN
Uh...

OLD WOMAN
Let's get a divorce.

Old Man sinks back into bed. He pulls the covers over his face. He starts to cry, contained at first, then louder and louder, like maybe he's having a bit of a meltdown.

OLD WOMAN

Shit.

OLD MAN

I'm no good. I'm useless.

Old Woman tries to comfort her husband but isn't quite sure what to do with her hands.

OLD WOMAN

No. You're not useless.

OLD MAN

Thank you.

OLD WOMAN

You're just clueless.

OLD MAN
(inconsolable)
That's the same thing!

OLD WOMAN

Do you want me to rub your belly?

Silence from under the covers.

OLD MAN

No.

Old Woman rubs anyway.

OLD WOMAN

Do you feel better?

OLD MAN

Are you really going to divorce me?

OLD WOMAN
Probably.

OLD MAN
I see.

OLD WOMAN
It's for the best. We could start dating again. Wouldn't that be fun?

OLD MAN
I guess. Maybe.

OLD WOMAN
Definitely.

OLD MAN
But then again, dating was the single most stressful thing I ever had to do in my entire life.

Old Woman stops rubbing.

OLD MAN
I mean – let's face it – neither of us had any moves.

OLD WOMAN
You were always wearing turtlenecks. You had a Beatles haircut.

OLD MAN
And you always ate with your mouth open.

Old Man emerges from the covers. He looks at his wife with melancholy.

OLD WOMAN
You're right. Dating in our twenties was terrible. So many horrendous first dates. So much bad breath and clammy hands.

OLD MAN
Maybe what we need is companionship.

OLD WOMAN
What do you mean?

OLD MAN
We could just be those kinds of divorced couples who aren't in love anymore, but they're still best friends.

OLD WOMAN
You're not my best friend.

OLD MAN
What?

OLD WOMAN
My best friend is Betty.

OLD MAN
Who the hell is Betty?!

OLD WOMAN
She's the lady that runs the bingo at the community center. She's my favourite person in the entire world. I love the way she says B-I-N-G-O.

OLD MAN
WHAT?!

OLD WOMAN
I'm sorry – did you not know that?

OLD MAN
I thought I was your best friend. I thought I was your favourite person in the world.

A deeply awkward silence.

OLD WOMAN
Oh, I'm sorry.

OLD MAN
Oh my God.

OLD WOMAN
I thought you knew.

OLD MAN
Well, now I kind of want a divorce.

Old Woman seems pleased by this.

OLD WOMAN
OK! So it's decided then. We're getting a divorce.

OLD MAN
Sounds good to me.

They turn on their sides almost at the same time, facing away from each other now like two sides of a broken cookie.

OLD WOMAN
But then again…

OLD MAN
Woman, make up your mind.

OLD WOMAN
(slow motion)
Excuse me?

OLD MAN
(instantly regrets it)
Never mind.

OLD WOMAN
If we get divorced, who would end up doing the paperwork?

OLD MAN
Forget I said anything.

OLD WOMAN
I'll give you a hint. Me. It would be me.

OLD MAN
Seems like an awful lot of work.

OLD WOMAN
Sure does – and I'm not getting any younger!

OLD MAN
I'm tired.

The couple turn once again onto their backs. They resume looking up at the ceiling.

OLD WOMAN
Maybe we should just not bother. I'm too old for this.

OLD MAN
OK.

OLD WOMAN
Let's re-evaluate the relationship in ten years. Deal?

OLD MAN
Deal.

OLD WOMAN
Until then, we'll just stay married.

                    OLD MAN
    OK.

                    OLD WOMAN
    Goodnight, then.

                    OLD MAN
    OK.

Old Man peels over to turn off the lamp.

Darkness.

Jade Tremblay grew up in Vancouver, Canada. She decided to write scripts because it was cheaper than therapy. Over the years she has come to realise the best way for her to write is to take unfortunate events in her own life and attempt to inject them with humour.

AMY WHITINGTON

The Clockmaker's Wife

The clicking and winding of gears can be heard from all around. It grows louder until it is almost unbearable.

The sound stops, replaced by the ticking of two clocks, slightly out of time, so that they resemble the beating of a heart.

The lights come up on the CLOCKMAKER's workshop. Every wall is covered in clocks; none of them appears to be working.

Every surface is covered in ancient clockwork toys, half-built and long neglected.

The CLOCKMAKER himself is a small, bald man of about 60 who squints behind his glasses. He is blind to almost everything that is not right in front of his nose. He sits bent far over a worktable centre-stage and works minutely on his project.

On the table is something that resembles a brass skeleton of human size. She is partially clad in gleaming plates. Where she is unclad, in her chest and stomach, her mechanical entrails are visible.

At length, the CLOCKMAKER's son CHARLIE enters. He is a mild young man approaching 30. He also wears glasses.

He spots his father and looks fondly if sadly at his back. He starts to say something, but doesn't. He crosses to a shelf and picks up a plateless pocketwatch.

CLOCKMAKER	What's missing?
CHARLIE	Escape wheel.

The CLOCKMAKER grunts in satisfaction.

>Should I fix it?

CLOCKMAKER	It's not broken.
CHARLIE	It's not?
CLOCKMAKER	I needed it.

>Good size. Nobody makes that size anymore.

CHARLIE looks at the watch for a moment, then checks to make sure his father's back is turned before pocketing it.

CHARLIE I had a... a bent balance wheel come in this morning. Funny, it must have been like that for years but the poor lady hadn't noticed. It took me a while to spot it, you would have seen it right away, but it was very slight. *Very* slight. I imagine she dropped it some years ago, or maybe had it serviced by some roadside mountebank, because for years, she said, she's been turning up later and later to church with no idea why.

Papa, I have news.

Papa, will you look at me? It's important and I'd rather not say it to the back of your head. I imagine it'll come as something of a surprise. Please don't think I was hiding it from you, just being cautious. Waiting for the right time. I thought you might approve of that. I wanted

	things to be certain, absolutely certain before I brought you the news. Will you turn around?
CLOCKMAKER	The only obvious solution.
CHARLIE	Sorry?
CLOCKMAKER	Bent balance wheel. Lost time. The only obvious solution.
CHARLIE	Papa...
CLOCKMAKER	Put the watch back.

CHARLIE obediently takes the watch from his pocket and goes to place it back on the shelf. He stops, looks at the back of his father's head and puts the watch back in his pocket.

CHARLIE	How is... it going?

CHARLIE steps closer to the table where the CLOCKMAKER's project lies. He is repulsed by it.

CLOCKMAKER	The movement in the hand is catching. The parts age as fast as I can replace them. And now they are no longer making the wheels I need.
CHARLIE	I see.
CLOCKMAKER	If you would help me, I could keep up with the degeneration of the parts long enough to replace the wheels.
CHARLIE	Replacing the wheels would render most of this heart mechanism obsolete.
CLOCKMAKER	We replace and replace.

CHARLIE	Until the plates corrode and need recasting. Or another spring snaps, one of thousands, which must be located and replaced. By which time the standard size of wheels may well have changed again.
CLOCKMAKER	You don't care. You have said you won't help me. Why do I ask?
CHARLIE	Wheels might have become obsolete altogether by the time you've done all that.
CLOCKMAKER	If you were to help me again…
CHARLIE	Then who would mind the shop? Who would be left to mend bent balance wheels? You don't go out front at all anymore. People have stopped asking after you. They must think you're…
	Papa. I'm getting married.
	She came in with a crooked pinion and I fixed it. The next day she came back and she brought croissants. We shared them on the counter, I thought if you caught me eating at the counter there'd be trouble. This was years ago. It took years.
	She's not young. She's… sad. I know she was married before.
	Papa, will you turn around? Her name's Clara, she sells pastries. Papa, will you..? I wanted to tell you because… Look at me. Because I'm going to live with her and I want… we want you to… we could look after you but the shop would have to… do you understand?

I can't leave you here on your own.

Papa, look at me.

Look at me!

LOOK AT ME!

CHARLIE takes his father's shoulder and then immediately lets go as though shocked by electricity. By his own boldness. He cradles his hand.

The CLOCKMAKER slowly turns, raises his head and squints in his son's direction.

CLOCKMAKER   And what would you have me do with your mother?

Beat.

CHARLIE   Please don't call it that.

CLOCKMAKER   I do not need looking after. I am looking after her.

CHARLIE   Papa, you can't run the shop on your own and I can't start my married life with Clara like this. Not here with… *that.*

CLOCKMAKER   She gave you life, doesn't she deserve the same in return?

CHARLIE   That is not my mother.

    Do you understand? I have to get you out of here. It has to stop. I want to help you.

CLOCKMAKER   You used to help me.

CHARLIE I was a child. I believed you. I'd never learned the difference between broken and… and… dead!

You'll like her. She wants to meet you. Please.

Please.

CHARLIE waits as long as he can. His father stares at the floor. Finally CHARLIE goes to leave, but just as he reaches the door, the CLOCKMAKER calls out to him.

CLOCKMAKER Charlie, put it back.

CHARLIE takes the watch from his pocket.

CHARLIE It was mother's. This was the one you made for her when you got married.

CLOCKMAKER Put it back.

CHARLIE And now you're butchering it for parts.

CLOCKMAKER She'll understand.

CHARLIE She'll understand.

That thing will consume everything eventually. It's already got you.

CLOCKMAKER How can you say such a thing?

The CLOCKMAKER tenderly takes his creation's hand.

CHARLIE She's just a movement.

CLOCKMAKER She is movement perfected.

CHARLIE   What's the problem then? After 18 years why doesn't she work? Did you forget to wind her?

CLOCKMAKER   It's the heart mechanism. It beats but…

CHARLIE   It's not beating, it's ticking.

CLOCKMAKER   *(Muttering)* The mainspring, the ratchet. The barrel has teeth. The teeth drive the centre wheel.

He holds his hand over her stomach.

               The wheel-train amplifies the force, the pinions catch, the nerves awaken. The wheels, fourth, fifth, thousands, the keyless-work, setting the mind to the moment she left.

He holds his hand over her face.

               Escapement with every tick of the balance wheel, that's the rhythm… Just like life. Perfect, accurate. Releasing. Releasing just one tooth by one. The lever pushes the balance wheel, it catches. A million pulses beat in time.

He takes her wrist and holds it up.

               Oscillating. Balanced. Delicate. Alive.

CHARLIE   Papa, please…

CLOCKMAKER   Her heart is beating but she won't wake. If the wheels catch.

               No.

The wheel catches. The lever pushes the balance… Each ventricle a mainspring. The mainspring is held by a ratch… a ratchet. By a.

It can't be done.

A heart cannot function on clockwork. I've tried for years. A heart cannot function on clockwork. I've tried a million combinations. I cannot feel my fingers. I cannot see.

Charlie, she won't wake up.

CHARLIE   Come with me. We can just leave!

He stays put.

CLOCKMAKER   She won't wake up.

The CLOCKMAKER gets off his stool and crosses to the side of the room where he wipes his oily hands on a rag and breaks down crying.

CHARLIE starts to cross to his father, but stops as he passes the creation. He gazes at her.

CHARLIE   I remember when I was eleven. When you took me upstairs – I hadn't seen you for days – and you showed me the plans. You said we could rebuild her. I helped you. I thought maybe we were all made of metal inside.

I fix a watch now and all I see are so many glittering entrails. The ticking and winding. It repulses me. Like the grinding of teeth. The cracking of knuckles. I feel the snap of a spring as though it were a tendon. I can't stay here.

He looks again at the watch in his hand and puts it back in his pocket.

> I wish I could remember what my mother's face looked like. I try to. I close my eyes and all I see is brass. Your monster took that, too.

CHARLIE picks up a hammer from the worktable and tests it in his hand. He thinks about it for a long time and then he raises his arm high.

> It has to die.

The dead clocks on the wall start to spring to life. The deafening call of a cuckoo bursts through the small room. Previously stationary machine parts now whirr and click, the ticking drowns everything. The lights flicker.

The CLOCKMAKER launches himself across the room and grabs CHARLIE's arm.

They struggle, CHARLIE eventually breaks free and smashes the clockwork heart.

The CLOCKMAKER roars, removes the hammer from his son and strikes him savagely across the face, knocking him to the floor.

Silence. The clockwork heart has stopped.

The CLOCKMAKER sinks to his knees and cradles the broken doll, sobbing pitifully. CHARLIE, clutching his face, gets to his feet.

CHARLIE   *Papa.*

CLOCKMAKER   It's just the mainspring. The escape wheel here, see, it's intact. We can start again. My darling. The wheel train can be replaced, my love. I just need more parts.

Appalled, CHARLIE leaves.

I can fix you.

I can fix you.

My love, I can fix you.

Lights down.

Amy Whitington is a graduate of a BA in English and History at the University of Southampton, and has been writing, directing and acting for the amateur stage since childhood. After temping for canteens, hospitals and offices, Amy decided to re-enter education and came to Norwich to study at UEA.